THE
LOST PC
OF CORNV

TOR MARK PRESS · REDRUTH

The Tor Mark series

First published 1994 by Tor Mark, PO Box 4, Redruth, Cornwall, TR16 5YX
This reprint with corrections 2002

ISBN 0-85025-345-4

Acknowledgements
The photographs are reproduced by kind permission of the Royal Institution
of Cornwall, except that on page 19 which is by kind permission of the
Cornwall Local Studies Library, Redruth.
The cover is a print by William Daniell, kindly lent by Mssrs John Maggs of Falmouth,
and shows Portreath – but has been reversed for design purposes.

Printed in Great Britain by R Booth (The Troutbeck Press) Mabe, Penryn, Cornwall

Introduction

Until the arrival of the railways changed the ancient patterns of trade, Cornwall depended on the sea for its transport. Roads and wheeled transport were virtually unknown in west Cornwall until the late eighteenth century, but there were many rivers, creeks and coves where small craft could put in and come close to the mineral workings. Even during the Industrial Revolution, when engineers were creating canal systems in the Midlands and north of England, Cornwall for all its significance as a centre of industry at that time had little need of canals because its small ports were quite adequate.

But ships were becoming larger, and at the same time the rivers were silting up as a result of waste from tin workings. This was no new problem. Lostwithiel was from 1200 to 1350 the most important port in Cornwall, and indeed the value of its trade made it second only to Southampton along the whole south coast; but silting had ruined it by 1400. By Henry VIII's time several more ports were all but lost. Grampound had long been useless and Tregony, once the major port of the Fal area and able to accept ships above 200 tons, was terminally silted by 1530. Many more were to disappear in the same way, choked by the debris of the very industry which had made them flourish.

Yet others continued in use until the twentieth century, suitable for schooners and other small coasting craft though often inaccessible at certain stages of the tide or in bad weather, and perhaps depending on quaint loading methods as at Tintagel, Trevaunance or Boscastle. For the most part they failed only when the industries they served failed – but perhaps in the end their inefficiencies added to the cost of transport and contributed to the failure of the industries.

Today their remains are often fascinating to explore, and these photographs will help you visualise them in their heyday. We have concentrated on those ports which could take vessels of 150 tons or more, omitting those harbours such as Newlyn or Mevagissey where fishing predominated, and largely ignoring the river quays which were numerous on the rivers Fal, Truro, Fowey and Tamar.

Today's major Cornish ports are Par and Fowey for the export of chine clay, Falmouth which because of its distance from the great industrial areas of Britain has never realised the potential of its wonderful harbour but concentrated on supplying and repairing ships and oil rigs, and in a smaller way Penzance, which has filled in most of its harbour to form a car park. Padstow hovers on the brink of making a comeback: we have included it because its history is interesting, and wish it success so that it can be omitted from the next edition of this book!

Bude

Until 1820 Bude hardly existed: it came into being because there was a demand for sea-sand to manure the agricultural hinterland. Small quantities of sand had been taken inland for centuries, but in 1819 an Act was passed allowing construction of the Bude Canal, which terminates in a sea-lock on the foreshore. It was unusual among canals in being built for an agricultural rather than a manufacturing purpose. The industrial buildings alongside the canal remain, but it is hard to imagine the bustle of activity which was normal there in Victorian times, as lighters were loaded with sand, and schooners awaited high tide to allow them through the lock.

The names, home ports and masters of all sixteen vessels in this photograph are known: nine of them are from Bideford, four from Padstow, and one each from Liverpool, Plymouth and Southampton.

Boscastle

The pier is said to have been rebuilt twice before 1584, when the present pier was built by Sir Richard Grenville; this was restored in 1740. It was always virtually impossible to sail out of the harbour: instead, a 'hobbling boat' rowed out with the 'warping rope', dropped an anchor with a pulley and brought the other end of the rope back. The shore party then hauled on the rope, thus pulling the ship out towards the anchor.

Manganese ore from near Launceston was shipped in the early nineteenth century, and in 1861 considerable quantities of iron ore from Trebursye, also near Launceston, were apparently being shipped from Boscastle. Later there was some china clay trade. Until 1920, 90 ton cargo boats from Appledore, the *Lively* and the *Bedoe*, regularly brought coal, manure and iron.

In the winter of 1848-9 a Mr Fuggard had paths prepared, with seats in the most picturesque positions, for the benefit of the visitors who were by then coming for the sake of their health or for the scenery.

Tintagel

Of all the improbable ports mentioned in this book, Tintagel may be the most surprising, since the cliffs are sheer and there is no immediate indication of a harbour. Yet in 1583 Sir Richard Grenville reported that there was room for four or five of the largest ships to embark or disembark troops. Later, slate was quarried nearby and vessels beached themselves in the cove to be loaded by derricks from wooden staging projecting from the cliff, and there was a mine here also.

Slate from the Delabole quarry, south of Tintagel, used also to be shipped from Port Gaverne (see page 31) and from Trebarwith Strand.

Archaeologists now believe that Tintagel was a Dark Age stronghold, not a monastery as previously thought, and that occasional ships from the Mediterranean landed their cargoes of wine and oil near the 'Iron Gate'.

Wadebridge

River access to Wadebridge was possible but not easy. Schooners could reach the town quays but could not get back down-river fully laden, so they would partially load and a barge would accompany them down-river with the rest of the cargo, to complete the loading when they reached Padstow.

Wadebridge had a steam railway very early – in 1833, when it was only the second in Britain. Sea-sand, for improving soil quality, was taken inland and granite brought back from the De Lank quarries. Iron ore and some china clay were also shipped out. These days the mineral traffic all goes by road and it is increasingly difficult to remember Wadebridge ever was a port.

Newquay

The original medieval harbour was in use by 1396. It enclosed a tiny area and could only take a vessel up to 80 tons, not being intended for trade but as a harbour of refuge; trading ships would unload in the Gannel or at Porth beach. The 'New Quay' was built in the mid sixteenth century mainly for fishing, although there was also some trade in ore but, according to Carew writing about 1600, the quay project was incomplete at that time.

The harbour was developed in the early 1800s, and a tramway was completed in 1849; it was initially horsedrawn. The purpose of the harbour and railway development was to transport ore from mines in the St Austell area to the smelters in South Wales, and china clay to the Potteries, without the long and dangerous journey round Land's End. The tramway ended at the Whim (the

present Somerfield supermarket) from where a tunnel leads down to the Aquarium, and this housed an inclined plane. From this point trucks trundled along a substantial timber jetty (demolished in 1950) onto the stone jetty which now sits isolated in the middle of the harbour.

There were four shipbuilding yards, making mostly small vessels, but one built a 230 ton craft in 1929. At its peak, Newquay owned 150 schooners, most of its 2000 population being shareholders in them, and was large enough to run its own maritime insurance company.

In 1876, a shortage of mineral traffic led to the railway being opened to passengers, which in turn led to the growth of Newquay as a tourist resort. The harbour became obsolete because the town was unwilling to extend the quays for steamers. At its peak the port could accommodate vessels up to 600 tons.

St Agnes/Trevaunance

The rationale for attempting to build a harbour here was to provide a north coast port for Truro, instead of using the beach at Perranporth or the Gannel at Newquay. According to the historian Polsue, 'An attempt was made by the Tonkin family in 1632 to form a harbour at Trevaunance-Porth; and again in 1684, but after a considerable outlay it was abandoned. A third attempt was made by Mr Hugh Tonkin in 1699, assisted by Winstanley the engineer. This was attended by some little success; but in 1705 it was completely destroyed by a storm.'

But nothing deterred the Cornish in those days. Rebuilding in 1710 cost £6000 and the work was destroyed in 1736. A further effort in 1794 cost £10,000; the result was a miniature harbour at the foot of the cliffs, on which was 'a crazy old wooden staging' from which the loading and unloading was carried out. 'A trade is carried on with Ireland, Wales, etc in lime, coal and slate.' The main trade was always bringing coal for the mines.

Cable Railway, Forneau

Portreath

The success of the local copper mining industry in the eighteenth century dictated the need for a local port, since copper ore had to be transported to South Wales for smelting and land transport was out of the question. A pier was commenced in 1760.

The pier, basin, jetty and warehouses cost £12,000, but before long a further £6000 was spent on the inner basin, more buildings, and roads. A small artillery battery protected Portreath from privateers: this had been erected in the American War, due to a daring attack made by an American privateer after some merchantmen had taken refuge in the bay. The attack was resisted by local people, allegedly armed only with 'fowling pieces'.

A tramway from Portreath to the mines in the St Day area started operating as far as Scorrier in 1812; this was the first railway (or technically, plateway) in Cornwall.

By 1840, 100,000 tons of copper ore a year were passing through Portreath, as well as imports of huge quantities of building materials and coal. In May 1873 twenty vessels laden with coals, three of them steamers, were in the harbour at once and further arrivals had to be diverted, but this was clearly exceptional. There was a yard building sailing vessels, and a shipping firm which owned eighteen schooners.

Portreath survived longer than most of the little ports but by 1950 only occasional colliers unloaded domestic fuel.

Padstow

Padstow's importance has been historically variable, depending until the nineteenth century on the amount of trade with Ireland. Possibly in the period after the departure of the Romans the level of trade was significant, and the town claims its origin from that time, although some historians believe that Rock was then of greater significance than Padstow. In the later middle ages there was little Irish trade but as English attempts to colonise Ireland increased in Elizabethan times, so trade increased and Padstow prospered.

Then in the eighteenth century a new trade developed, no longer dependent on Ireland. Copper ore and refined tin were shipped out, as were slates and farm produce; timber, coal, salt and many other products were imported.

Dr Pococke, an Irish bishop visiting in 1750, wrote: 'At Padstow is a pretty good mole, but there is a large bar, at the western end of which there is a very narrow entrance to the harbour. They have a trade to Ireland in corn, and to Bristol for many goods, and to Wales for coal; and they have a trade in the fine light slates of Delabole, which are brought to it from Port Isaac.'

In 1862 quarrying began at Stepper Point, in order to improve the wind at the mouth of the estuary; previously it was so turbulent and confusing that a capstan was erected on Stepper Point to haul ships in. In the late 19th century there would be 40 or 50 cargo ships waiting to unload, but trade gradually fell away.

Tradition has it that an ill-treated mermaid had condemned the port to be overcome with sand. By 1950 the harbour was so silted up that no ship could float at low tide, but some coal boats up to 800 tons still used it. That was its low point. Today there are strenuous efforts to make the port viable again, with steady dredging and a throughput of over 600,000 tons, so Padstow is no longer a 'lost port' but is rapidly refinding itself.

Hayle

Hayle's success was initially founded on the smelting of copper, demanding massive imports of coal; this had ceased by 1806 because it was found more economical to smelt the ore in South Wales. But there was a continuing export of copper ore and tin. The next development was Harvey's Foundry, which imported iron and fuel and exported finished products. In 1842, for example, the foundry despatched 1800 tons of ironwork to construct Clifton suspension bridge. The foundry later turned to iron shipbuilding and at one time it employed a thousand people.

The channel by which shipping approached Hayle was formed by the Cornish Copper Company in 1769 but vessels over 70 tons could not enter on account of the obstruction caused by shifting sands. In 1788 an embankment was built across the mouth of Phillack Creek: the pent-up water was released in a rush at low tide to flush away the sand. Further improvements were made and by 1870 shipping of 250 tons could approach the quays.

A regular steamship service to Bristol was established in the 1830s and, until the through rail link to London was established in 1859, Hayle thrived on exports to Bristol for onward shipment by rail to London. The completion of the railway, the decline of the mining industry and the impossibility of accommodating large modern ships in a shallow estuary combined to reduce activity at the port.

St Ives

The first stone pier was not built until nearly 1500, but St Ives was probably the foremost Cornish fishing port in the middle ages. It also imported timber and beef from Ireland and charcoal from Wales. In the seventeenth century the growth of copper and tin mining in the area, and an increased local population demanding a wide variety of goods, put a strain on the harbour facilities.

The pier was replaced with a larger one in 1770 but the harbour dried out at low tide, so was not of use to large vessels; nevertheless there was a direct trade to Italy with pilchards, returning with Spanish fruit, direct importation of hides from South America and timber from the Baltic, coal from South Wales and coastal trade to Bristol. Smuggled goods were also substantial.

The last cargo boat brought coal in 1935.

St Michael's Mount

If, as is thought, St Michael's Mount is the island of 'Iktis' described by ancient writers, from which the Cornish exported their tin, then it can claim to be one of Cornwall's earliest ports.

The pier was rebuilt about 1428 by the monks on the Mount, after attempts to raise money in Marazion had failed, and the governors of the Mount were responsible for its upkeep. It was greatly improved in the mid eighteenth century and its entrance enlarged in 1823 to accommodate vessels up to 500 tons. Probably in good weather ships chose to unload on the beach at Marazion, but they would not have made this their destination if they had not been able to rely on the protection of the harbour if a storm blew up, since Mount's Bay is a highly dangerous lee shore.

Porthleven

The mines of Breage, Germoe and Wendron were among the most active in Cornwall, and Porthleven seemed ideally placed to act as their port, especially when Gweek was silting up. There was an Act in 1811 to enable the harbour to be improved and much money was expended, but the attempt was a failure. Harveys of Hayle took the project over in 1855 and by building a lock made the port available to light shipping, and far safer for the fishing fleet.

The cove faces south-west, into the worst of the gales, and it is not surprising that the breakwaters often suffered damage, and indeed still do. It was also very difficult of access for sailing craft and never attracted any significant trade.

Nevertheless it was home to a large fishing fleet, as this old photograph shows, despite the poor condition of the negative.

Porthoustock

An attractive village, hiding on the east side of the Lizard peninsula, 'Proustock' as it is locally pronounced was a fishing hamlet until the opening up of a roadstone quarry in the 1890s. The massive loading facility is still highly visible, and the beach was mainly built up with debris from the quarry, which closed in 1958.

Since it was noisy, dirty and industrial during the period when tourism was fast developing, Porthoustock has remained all but unaffected by it.

Gweek

Visitors to the famous seal sanctuary may be unaware that they are at one of Britain's most ancient ports, which was trading tin to Spain in 450 BC. The Roman camp nearby at Grambla suggests it was still in use in Roman times.

Gweek was active as the port of Helston in the middle ages, but only for trading within Britain, as it does not appear in the national customs records.

In the Tudor period it was very active, since local tin smelting was thriving. Even in the 1860s, Polsue could say: 'Gweek is a sea-port situated on Helford harbour; and from it Helston, the adjacent country and the mines are supplied with coals, lime, timber and other merchandise. The exports consist of copper ore, granite, corn, pilchards and oysters. A pilchard fishery is also established here; and at various times great quantities of herrings have been taken.'

Later, ships bringing timber were unloaded downstream into barges which were able to reach Gweek, or alternatively the timber was formed into rafts and poled up to Gweek on the rising tide.

Penryn

The town was founded in 1216 by Simon de Apulia, an Italian who was bishop of Exeter. In the middle ages it did comparatively little trade, but developed as a victualling port, with good supplies of corn from no less than four mills, and copious fresh water. Many ships called here for supplies, either before their outward voyage or on arrival from the Atlantic, before completing the voyage to London, Antwerp or the Baltic.

Like Truro it was important when ships were too small for the more exposed waters of Falmouth. The late seventeenth century was its heyday, with many schooners alongside Exchequer Quay; contrary to popular belief the development of Falmouth did not damage Penryn's trade, which actually increased, due to exports of granite and tin, imports of coal, charcoal, timber and manufactured goods for the mining hinterland. Until the development of Devoran around 1820, Penryn handled most of this trade.

In addition to this, a trade began to flourish with the American colonies, imports of tobacco and exports of all the general products which could be made more cheaply in England, everything from socks to clay pipes.

Granite for dockyards, lighthouses, London bridges and Irish churches became highly significant in the early nineteenth century, and by this time the shipowners of Penryn had regular shipping routes to London (six vessels), Plymouth and the Solent. The photograph was taken in 1855.

Cattle were imported here from Spain in the late nineteenth century, and forced to swim ashore to save quarantining them – it being supposed that salt water would act as a disinfectant. This trade was stopped because sometimes foul winds and a slow passage led to their arriving in poor condition.

Truro

The city came into existence as a tin port, at the lowest point where the rivers could be bridged or forded. One problem for historians is that records speak of Falmouth when no such town existed: they intend the whole of the Fal estuary. When tin is concerned, 'Falmouth' should almost certainly be taken to mean Truro which was the coinage town. 'Truro harbour' included the town quays, Calenick, Malpas, Newham Quay, Mylor, Round Wood Quay, Tresillian, Perran Wharf, Devoran and Point.

Truro merchants were in the carrying trade by Tudor times, for example carrying woollen cloth from Wales to Brittany and wine from Bordeaux back to Wales, as well as Welsh coal to Devon and Cornwall. It was the development of larger ships in the seventeenth century, rather than the growth of Falmouth, which led to the decline in Truro's trade, but the town's importance as a commercial and industrial centre and a tin-exporter was so great that the quays were still well used, even though transhipment to lighters was necessary.

There were objections in 1848 to the building of Boscawen Bridge, because vessels with fixed masts, of up to 60 tons, had until then been able to reach the town quays. (What would they have said to the river being covered at Lemon Quay and turned first into a car park and more recently into a piazza?) Trade continued with vessels of up to 500 tons unloading at Malpas into lighters, which had either lugsails on short masts or masts which could be unstepped.

Until early Victorian times there was a shipbuilding yard on Lemon Quay, producing sloops and schooners for coastal trade.

During the 1939-45 war much use was made of the deep water facilities of the Fal River; they are still used to 'mothball' large merchant ships and tankers.

Devoran

As many as thirty vessels at a time were to be seen at Devoran (opposite) at the peak of copper production in the Gwennap mines. It was the terminus of the Redruth & Chasewater Railway, officially opened in 1826 and horse-drawn until 1854. The trains carried ore down from the mines and coal back up, both in huge quantities. But in 1870 a collapse in metal prices was wrecking the mining industry and Devoran was nearly deserted. By 1877 the train made only one journey a day and there was no traffic to the port, yet somehow both railway and port continued until 1915.

Charlestown

The St Austell area in the last quarter of the eighteenth century suddenly acquired great industrial significance. The tin and copper mines were booming and a new industry – china clay – grew out of nothing. But St Austell had no harbour, only the open beach and rocky cove at West Polmear. Charles Rashleigh was the first to seize this opportunity.

He built Charlestown within twenty years, carving out the rock of the cove with teams of men using picks and shovels and bringing his water supply eight miles from Luxulyan in an aqueduct. The port is still there almost as he built it, and eminently attractive, but its great days are long gone, when the tiny harbour was notorious for overcrowding and delays, as here in 1914. After a sequence of owners during the early 1990s the harbour is now in the hands of Square Sail, a company committed to preserving the character of the village and the waterside, and the harbour's future looks secure.

The shipwreck museum contains interesting local history as well as shipwreck exhibits, including *Titanic* artifacts, and is well worth a visit.

Pentewan

Pentewan (opposite) was Charlestown's rival, built by Sir Christopher Hawkins. It was in business as a china clay port by 1826. A railway was opened from St Austell in 1829. Pentewan quickly outstripped Charlestown but silting of the harbour was always a problem. In 1862 the sandbanks shifted and 16 small ships were trapped in the port for well over a month. It was not unknown for the harbour mouth to disappear completely – as it has today. It finally closed in 1918.

Looe

The bustling fish quay gives the impression today of a thriving port, yet it is a pale reflection of the trade and relative prosperity of Looe in the past, when East and West Looe between them returned four members of parliament.

Medieval Looe had five of its own ships in the wine trade with Bordeaux by 1310, but later it declined and most of its trade until the nineteenth century was small and varied, including iron, tin, lead, fish, fish-oil, wine, soap, cloth and canvas, corn and tobacco. There was also much activity carrying sea sand and lime for inland soil improvement.

A rapid growth of the port followed the opening of the Looe Canal in 1828, serving the various mines and quarries north of Liskeard. Subsequent discoveries of copper ore, re-opening of the lead mines and new granite quarries brought a flurry of activity, so much so that the wharfs had to be extended in the 1860s. Both these photographs date from 1904.

Looe shipped out granite from the quarries near Minions, initially brought by railway to Moorswater in Liskeard and transhipped onto the canal, then later by rail all the way when the canal was filled in. It was despatched to London to construct Westminster Bridge, and all along the south coast to build forts, docks and breakwaters.

River Tamar, Calstock

Calstock and the Tamar quays

The Tamar was always Cornwall's largest navigable river and Calstock had a quay in Saxon times. Its greatest prosperity began with the success of local copper mining in the 1770s: in its heyday the quays stretched for nearly a mile, and an inclined plane (the remains of which are still visible) connected with a railway running to Kelly Bray. Copper ore and granite formed the main part of the trade.

The railway viaduct was completed in 1908, and it was no longer necessary to use the inclined plane, the Calstock wharfs, or even the Tamar. Calstock as a port did not collapse immediately because the town had many other industries to fall back on, but its days were numbered.

Of the other old quays on the river, Morwellham on the Devon side was the port of Tavistock and is now part of the museum; Cotehele Quay has also been preserved, by the National Trust, and houses an old river barge; Halton and Cargreen are also of interest and Landulph – now some way from the river – was a significant port in the Middle Ages.

Some notable omissions

Port Isaac and Port Gaverne: Port Isaac was never accessible to shipping over 100 tons, whereas in the 1860s 'Port Gaverne has a considerable business in the shipping of slate from Delabole Quarries and occasionally the importation of coals from Wales.' The ships were simply beached alongside the wall. The slate was exported from both these little ports to Plymouth, Falmouth, Padstow and

Barnstaple for onward shipment; it was loaded by a chain of women into the ships' holds and packed with hay. Limestone, coal, manure and grain were imported. The trade was ruined when the railway reached Delabole.

Lelant: Quays were constructed in 1876 just prior to the construction of the railway to St Ives. Vessels drawing 17ft could approach at full tide. A new cart road was built at the same time but Cornwall was immediately thrown into economic depression and the port never began to succeed.

Mousehole was probably an older port than Penzance or Newlyn. Primarily a fishing community, Mousehole nevertheless exported cured fish train oil and woollen cloth to the English garrisons of Gascony in the fourteenth century and brought back salt for fish curing. Its breakwater was the earliest in Cornwall, begun in 1393. Small cargo ships visited it until about 1900.

Newlyn: At no time was it a major trading port, having concentrated highly successfully on its fishing industry. However, since the construction of the large harbour in the late nineteenth century, it has been possible to accommodate substantial vessels if necessary: in 1910 the 7500 ton SS *Lerdre* of Nantes put in. Roadstone was also exported from the Penlee quarries.

Mevagissey's pier was reconstructed in the 1770s and again in the 1860s. The fishing industry dominated its trade, with 80 fishing vessels registered there in the 1850s and much direct export from Mevagissey to Italy, but other trade did occur: hemp, tallow and iron were imported for the mines, and barrel staves for the pilchard industry. Some china clay was exported in the late nineteenth century.

Lerryn: The last boats to call were manure boats from Penryn, about 1930. The last surviving port official remembered a 200 ton craft coming in, probably in the late 1890s delivering coal.

Saltash was established in the late twelfth century as a seaport from which Dartmoor tin could be shipped, after being brought down-river from Tavistock. Saltash was made a borough about 1190 (the scribe forgot to date the charter) when it was named Esse. Esse and Fowey (meaning Lostwithiel) were at that time the only Cornish ports permitted to export, but its future was blighted by Plymouth from about 1260. Saltash was the mother port, but the child soon outgrew its mother.